Treasure Island:
the sequel

Other books in this series:

The Jingle Book
A Load of New Rubbish
Albert, the Lion and the Monkey
The Owl and the Pussycat
The Pied Pipe Man of Haslingden
The Stair Lift Olympics
The Tuneful Foghorns

Available from
The Book Case, 29 Market Street,
Hebden Bridge, West Yorks. HX7 6EU
or your local bookshop.

Treasure Island: the sequel

and other ludicrous lines

by

Chris Aspin

Very best wishes,

Chris Aspin

2013

RP

Published by Royd House
The Book Case
29 Market Street
Hebden Bridge
West Yorks.
HX7 6EU
www.bookcase.co.uk

Cover cartoon: Dick Graham

Cover design: D&P Design and Print

ISBN: 978-1-907197-12-3

CONTENTS

Gray's other elegy

Mr Gray, the English poet,
Sits beneath a jujube tree
In an elegiac graveyard
By a Middle Eastern sea.

In the distance cries the muezzin,
Calling all good folk to pray,
And before him sails a dhow man,
Weary at the close of day.

'Desert airs are full of sweetness.
They are very good for me,
Keeping colds at some great distance,
Leaving both my nostrils free.'

Now he reads the ancient tombstones
– Rumi, Saadi, O. Khayyám –
'Poets justly praised and famous
And much better than I am.

Still I did my best in Britain.
I admired the Common Man,
And I know that village-Hampdens
All appreciate my plan.

Do not mock my firm ambition
To escape the madding crowd.
Noble strife is now my motto.
Though I'm sunburned, I'm unbowed.'

The capture of Quebec

*[In 1759, during the Seven Years' War,
General James Wolfe read Thomas Gray's*
Elegy Written in a Country Churchyard *to
his officers on the night before the Battle of
the Plains of Abraham, afterwards
remarking, 'Gentlemen, I would rather
have written that poem than take Quebec
tomorrow.' Let us suppose that he did write
the poem and that Gray was sent to fight
the French.]*

The cuckoo sounds the dawning of the day.
The English poets have arrived by sea.
Their leader is the famous Mr Gray,
Who comes to make the fearsome French-
     men flee.

Far from the madding crowd's ignoble
     strife,
These rhymesters with their megaphones in
     hand,
Prepare, each one, to risk both limb and life
To foster freedom in this foreign land.

These strong campaigners, each with
     dauntless breast,
Their hearts all pregnant with celestial fire,
Prepare to show they are the very best
And that in combat they will never tire.

Mr Gray outlines his plan:

First a bombardment with Miltonic verse –
The lines that tell how Paradise was lost –
Then sonnet salvoes, razor-sharp and terse,
Next heavy odes and dirges cleanly tossed.

The French falter. The onslaught continues.

Now apt alliteration hits the foe
And epigrams destroy their will to fight.
'Mon Dieu!' the Frenchmen cry, and full of
        woe,
They flee the field of battle white with fright.

Stout English verse has gained this golden
        day;
And poets, mighty in their mastery,
In triumph homeward plod their cheery way
And leave the world to darkness with much
        glee.

The traveller

'Is there anybody there?
  said the traveller.
'I've just popped round
  for a chat.'
'We're all at home,'
  said the listeners.
'Now please wipe your
  boots on the mat.'

Expert opinion

'Why so glum?' asked Simple Simon.
    'Another birthday. They come round
far too often,' replied the Village Idiot.
    'Look on the bright side, old friend.
Remember what the experts tell us.'
    'Which ones?'
    'The statisticians. They've proved,
beyond all reasonable doubt, that people
with the most birthdays live the longest.'

Strange but true

[Passengers left 87,356 umbrellas on London Underground trains in 1934, the year records began. The figure for 2011 was 7,798.]

Everybody had a brolly
Back in 1934.
Many, though – those prone to folly –
Left theirs lying on the floor.
Heavy losses were reported
By the London Underground.
All were stored away and sorted:
Many hundreds, it was found.
Day by day the numbers mounted
At a rate that blew the mind.
Extra staff came in and counted
All umbrellas left behind.
Vast the total at the year end,
One that left the world transfixed:
Yes – eighty-seven thousand
Plus another three five six.

Sticking together

Adhesion! Adhesion! Now that must be our
    creed,
For sticking close together has become our
    biggest need.
We'll make the cautious cobbler stick firmly
    to his last
And lay in stocks of Super Glue and choice
    Elastoplast.
For clued up, glued up folk like us, there is
    no sticking point
And sticky wickets are no threat to put us
    out of joint.
To our tough tasks we'll firmly stick as every
    stickler should,
But never, never ever, will we stick into the
    mud.

The right track

So, you'd like to make much money
While you're young and in good health.
Learn to kick a football, sonny.
That's the ruthless road to wealth.

If, however, you'd much rather
Look back on a well-spent youth,
Take the track that leads you farther;
Take the one that leads to Truth.

The Red Brigade

If you're well read, you'll be aware
That fiery folk all have red hair,
And by a raw red-blooded law,
They all are red in tooth and claw.
Red letter days are never dull.
Each is a red rag to a bull.
They jump red lights; they sup red wine;
They call themselves the Thin Red Line.
They wave red flags; they throng Red
  Square;
They tread red carpets everywhere.
But caught red-handed when misled
By reds who hide beneath their bed,
They look red-faced with ruddy gape
As though entangled in red tape

Blue

Blue's a 'make your mind up' word,
Which for a colour's quite absurd.
Poets use it when they try
To paint the sea or cloudless sky.
Lovers, though, will often sing
Of their blue gloom and Cupid's sting.

Green

The lights turn green and off we go
To meadows where green grasses grow;
To gardens with green-fingered friends;
To bowling greens with well-trimmed ends.
Greengrocers in the town display
Their fruit and veg in green array
And in the greenhouse by the shed
The green tomatoes turn to red.
Green shoots are springing, sharp and
      clean,
To keep our country evergreen.
And look! The greenest sight you'll see:
Green-welly girls all fancy-free.

Wordsworth

Wordsworth was dour and down to earth,
Strong on valleys, groves and hills;
Rainbows, streams and daffodils,
But weak on mirth.

On the catwalk

Amarantha Knotworth-Waring,
Fashion writer feared by all,
Thinks the dress is far too daring;
Thinks the cut is too uncaring;
Thinks the buttons overbearing;
Says the whole thing's 'off the wall'.
Models on the catwalk tremble;
Damned designers all dissemble;
Boutique owners all resemble
Battered bruisers in a brawl.

When she chooses pink or yellow,
Those with blue and green all bellow;
Black and white will never mellow.
Amarantha's 'on the ball'.

November

November's here:
No hope of cheer;
No sun-warmed days;
No morning haze;
No leaves on trees;
No bumble bees;
No cuckoos' cries;
No butterflies;
No rise of larks;
No prams in parks;
No solar cells;
No bathing belles;
No cricket match;
No suntan patch;
No cooling drinks;
No flowering pinks;
Some sun today?
No. Not till May.

Quote ... unquote

Hail smiling morn, in russet mantle clad.
The sun shines brightly on the Shropshire
     Lad,
Who gazes at those blue remembered hills,
Glad he's divorced from dark satanic mills.
Beside the lake he wanders on his way,
Until he hears the knell of parting day.
The beauty of the morning; silent, bare,
Prompts him from time to time to stand and
     stare.
Surprised by joy, he reads the Highway
     Code,
Footloose upon the rolling English road.

'Oh, what a beautiful morning,' he cries.
'It makes me feel healthy and wealthy and
     wise.'

Quite soon the long day's journey sets alight
The sharp and hungry edge of appetite.
He sees the church clock stand at ten to
     three
And wonders, 'Is there honey still for tea?'
Afternoon tea-cakes, too, and buttered
     scones
To offer comfort to his tired bones.
Impatient as the wind, he hurries on
To reach his goal before the sun has gone.
Now home, rejoicing, what has he to say?
  'If you've the will, there always is a way.'

The politician

'Have you a soap box I could borrow?' asked Simple Simon.

'I don't use much soap,' replied the Village Idiot. 'Why do you want one?'

'I'm going into politics and need something to stand on when I address the electors.'

'I think I've an egg box.'

'That wouldn't do. Soap boxes are essential. I wouldn't get many votes standing on an egg box.'

'I'm sure the party of your choice has a good stock. The Tories have scented soap boxes. Labour are more carbolic.'

'I'm not joining either. I'm starting my own party – LAMP.'

'What's that?'

'The Laugh a Minute Party, inspired by that Italian comic, who polled so highly in the recent election. There's a great future in politics for comedians.'

'You're right there. The great leaders of the past weren't much fun. Think of Hitler, who hated the Jews because they could laugh at themselves, or Stalin, whose only pleasure was bumping people off. That Chinese bloke was a bit better. When somebody asked him about the effects of the French Revolution, he said it was too early to tell. Nice joke.'

'Don't be too sure. He probably meant it.'

'However, back to the soap box. I'm not convinced it's the right foundation for a comical party such as yours; far too hygienic.'

'What do you suggest, then?'

'How about a jack-in-the-box?'

'Why not? Great idea. I'll buy one this afternoon.'

Treasure Island: the sequel

The great detective, Ivor Clue,
Was asked to find a missing shoe.
It happened at a top hotel,
Where wealthy Mrs Wishingwell,
Distracted by a night of booze,
Threw off her footwear; took a snooze.
When she awoke beside the pool,
The shoe had gone, but not one jewel.
They called in Sherlock Holmes, but he
Said, 'This is much too big for me.
The only thing that you can do
Is send at once for Ivor Clue.'

The great detective quickly came
And said – his intellect aflame –
'The left one's gone, but here's the right:
A woman's, high-heeled, red and bright.
From this one fact, we can be sure
The thief is female, doubtless poor,
Fashion conscious, doubtless slim,
But lacking her right nether limb.
The substitute could be of wood
Or even cork and with a stud.'
And so a thorough search began,
Enormous in its scope and span,
Through regions often dark and shady,
To find the wanted peg-legged lady.

When searching proved to be defective,
Ivor Clue, the great detective,

Vowed the crime would be unmasked,
And thinking very hard, he asked,
'Who would a girl in such a state
Set out to capture for a mate?'
Long John Silver sprang to mind,
A fellow also realigned.
'A perfect pair,' the sleuth then cried,
'Our pressing task is simplified.
Treasure Island now must be
The focus of our fervency.'

Our story moves to southern seas,
The home of aborigines
And much to Ivor Clue's delight,
A figure he had hoped to sight:
A one-legged man bestride a boulder
With a parrot on his shoulder.
'Long John Silver?' 'Yes, that's my name.
A navigator known to fame.
I owe my moments in the sun
To Robert Louis Stevenson,
The author of the double-dyed
Romance of Jekyll and of Hyde.'

'I'm here,' declared the famous spook,
'To claim the shoe your girl friend took
One morning at the Ritz Hotel,
A place, I'm sure, you know quite well.'
The sea dog laughed; and then he said,
'Romance for me has long been dead.
I had a girl in every port,
When I was young, but not the sort

To make me want to settle down.
Perish the thought! I'd rather drown.
But I've good news to ease your pain:
Your prolonged quest's not been in vain.
I have the shoe of which you speak,
A specimen I think unique;
And it, I'm sure, should be returned
To that dear lady, who's concerned
To have it back so she can show
That she's again magnifico.'

'Let me explain,' the parrot squawked
(When in the mood, it often talked).
'I took the shoe to pull his leg.
I like to take him down a peg.
I visit London in all weathers
To deal in coloured fashion feathers,
And when I saw the silly shoe,
I thought, "Long John, this is for you".'
'I wore it once,' the sailor said,
'But just to please this featherhead.
The heel was far too high, alas,
And made me look too upper class,
Apologies to you, dear sir,
We must forgive when parrots err.'

'And I must do a U-turn, too,'
Declared the shamefaced Ivor Clue.
'How can I ever hope to thrive
When I think two plus two makes five?
I must confess I've been remiss.
(Smug Holmes must not get wind of this;

Nor Stevenson, for I would grovel,
If he unmasked me in a novel.)
Mum's the word. If you'll agree,
I'll give you my substantial fee.'

'No need for that,' replied Long John.
'And do not feel so woebegone.
Of course my parrot was to blame.
He thought his theft was just a game.
But birds all act upon a whim,
So we must not be hard on him.
I trust you'll learn from your mistake
That sleuthing is no piece of cake.
Now turning to your massive fee:
Give all of it to charity.
But first anonymously send
Your client costly shoes that blend
High fashion with the power to quell
Her rivals at the Ritz Hotel.'

But the parrot has the last word.

Suppose the lady wants to know
Who sent the shoes. Ho ho! Ho ho!
Suppose she sends for Ivor Clue.
What will the great detective do?

[Watch this space]

Experts (1)

They told us that the world was flat
And that it never moved.
Alas, these stories are old hat,
Derided and disproved.

Fresh experts claimed that our old earth
Goes round and round the sun,
And mentioned (just for what it's worth)
That it would run and run.

But now they tell us that this world
Will one day cease to be,
Burned by a blazing sun and hurled
Into infinity.

Experts (2)

Experts said that witches flew
On broomsticks with a cat or two
And then with Satan (in the nude)
Did things considered rather rude.
Dull magistrates, who disapproved,
Soon had these lively ladies moved
(It was, they said, for their own good)
To places where tall gallows stood.
'Well, I'll be hanged,' we say today,
As sorceresses freely play
In covens to their hearts' content
And with the government's consent.
Now witches sleep at ease at nights,
For pagans have their human rights.

Experts (3)

For years the experts understood
That ships were always made of wood.
Nobody ever dared to think
That iron ones would fail to sink.
Today we know that every boat
That's made of metal stays afloat.
What, indeed, could be much finer
Than an ocean-going liner?

Experts (4)

No aeroplane, the experts knew,
Could ever leave the ground.
A craft so heavy and its crew
Put flying out of bounds;
But how they changed their tiresome
    talk,
When Wil and Orville Wright
Took to the air at Kitty Hawk
And made the world's first flight.

Eminently quotable

Brush up your Shakespeare;
Start quoting him now.
There's plenty to cheer in Hamlet and Lear,
So add to the height of your brow.

'To be or not to be' you're sure to know
And 'All the world's a stage' is quite a hit.
Some people are 'as chaste as unsunned
      snow';
Brevity is the very soul of wit.
'The wheel is come full circle,' said the king,
Who called The Prince of Darkness quite a
      gent.
Immortal Hamlet cried, 'The play's the
      thing.'
He thought the morning air a pleasant
      scent.
'Ill met by moonlight' strikes a magic note;
'Sermons in stones' a phrase you'll not
      forget.
'This happy breed of men' is one to float.
'My kingdom for a horse' a sharp vignette.

Brush up your Shakespeare;
There are so many lines to pursue.
So quote from Othello, Macbeth and King
      Lear
And from King Henry the Fourth, Part
      Two.

Waves

Air waves or hair waves? Which one will you
 choose?
Each has its pitfalls, but both can amuse.
Think of the golden girl's garland of curls.
How it must please her and how her mind
 whirls,
But pity the legion of hapless young men,
Who fall for her ringlets again and again.

By the magic of wireless we're able to hear
The music of Mozart, the words of King
 Lear.
Alas, there is also much to displease:
Strange sounds of pop art, the words of
 MPs.

Companions

Said the lion to the unicorn
On the crest they ornamented,
'How very strange that I was born
And you were – well – invented.'

The gods

The gods, our ancient experts knew,
Controlled the world's affairs;
But though they always hid from view,
They sometimes heard the prayers.
And when the public didn't get
The things for which they prayed,
The high priest told them not to fret:
'The service is delayed.
The gods move in mysterious ways
Their wonders to perform.
If you are troubled by delays,
Consider it the norm.'
As years went by the public guessed
That something wasn't right.
The gods had clearly failed the test,
Each one a parasite.
Soon all the famous temples closed;
The sacrifices ceased.
The gods at last were all exposed;
The people had been fleeced.
From high Olympus crept the gods
To find another life.
They fought each day against great odds;
They felt the force of strife.
They're scattered far; their power has
          gone.
But since they are immortal,
They all must try to carry on
While lesser mortals chortle.
Old Neptune is a deck hand now;

Venus a cloistered nun.
(Who would have thought she'd take
        the vow
To say goodbye to fun?)
A postman with a rural round –
That's Mercury's disjunction.
His feet are firmly on the ground,
His wings no longer function.
Bacchus bottles fizzy water;
Cupid spends his days in bed;
Zeus is wanted for manslaughter;
Mars is living in a shed.
'There for the grace of God go I,'
An undertaker cried.
'How sad to see them such small fry;
Much better if they'd died.'

Moonstruck

The boffin said no one could go
In rockets to the moon,
But, as both you and I well know,
He spoke out far too soon.

In the beginning

Archbishop Ussher is our man;
He knows a thing or two.
He's worked out when the world
     began,
So honour where it's due.
October twenty-third the day,
Four thousand and four BC.
The exact hour he doesn't say,
But maybe ten to three.
That would allow the Lord to rest
In time for tea and toast.
He'd laboured hard and done His best
Helped by the Holy Ghost.

The prisoner

Pity the prisoner locked in his cell
And mocked by his jubilant gaoler.
Shackled and shocked; pale and unwell,
He feels his frail body grow frailer.

Alone in the dark and seeing no clock,
He thinks of the length of his sentence.
Each dawn he waits for the crow of a
     cock
And feels there's no point in repentance.

No thank you

'Will you to step into my whirlpool?'
Said the river to the schoolgirl.
'A swirl in such a torrent beats the sun.
Let my vortex hurl and curl you;
Be a spool and let me twirl you.
I warrant that the fair sex finds it fun.'

Said the cool girl to the river,
'I feel no need to quiver.
'Your whirling pool would make me most
        annoyed.
The shocks that you deliver
Would cause a shameful shiver
That any mocking schoolgirl would avoid.'

Children's corner

Now children, here's a motley crew
To act a pantomime for you.
So settle back and close your eyes
And watch the Dreamland curtain rise.
The first upon the empty stage
Is Rip Van Winkle in a rage,
For he's been wakened from his sleep
By Tom, the soot-stained chimney sweep,
Pursued (though guilty of no crimes)
By the egregious Mr Grimes.
'Your bawling,' Rip Van Winkle shouts,
'Is causing chaos hereabouts.'
Then seizing Grimes, he takes a shoe
And beats the fellow black and blue.
'Now Tom,' he says, 'since I'm awake,
I think that you and I will take
This happy chance to make our mark
By setting up a leisure park.
Some well-known people come this way
And they will be quite pleased to stay
A little while and at great charge,
For their vainglory's very large.'

> *Here comes one – a politician,*
> *Smirking as he tells his lies.*
> *Mark him out for demolition.*
> *He's the one to liquidize.*

'Well done, Tom,' cries Rip Van Winkle,
'That's the way to stop his tinkle.

And now he's gone to meet his maker,
Have you called the undertaker?

Next, children, you will shortly see
Two ugly sisters on a spree.
They want to find that handsome fella,
Who's run away with Cinderella.
They're very jealous of their sister
And would like to beat and twist her,
So when these dreadful dames appear,
Stand on your seats and boo and jeer;
Then take these cabbages and eggs
And hurl them at their heads and legs.

The harridans are back in panto;
And so we end our final canto.

What if ..?

What if the Moon is made of cheese?
What if, one day, a wayward breeze
Should carry it, all brown and round,
And drop it on the line of trees
That stands atop the rising ground
    Behind my house?

Would hungry men arrive with knives
And at some hazard to their lives,
Climb up the oaks and cut a slice?
And while the tasty cheese survives
Will it some bird or beast entice,
    Perhaps a mouse?

What if the world is really flat?
There seems to be much sense in that.
Some experts, though, say it's a sphere.
If that is so, I'll eat my hat.
I have no wish to live in fear
    Of falling off.

What if the world ends in a ledge
Surrounded by a privet hedge
Or by a wall of stone or brick
Impervious to any wedge
And very tall and very thick?
    Please do not scoff.

To baldly go

On Ilkley Moor without a hat!
Dear sir, you must not think of that.
The hill's a dreaded danger zone,
Where gales from Keighley freeze the bone
And Bradford breezes thick with fog
Leave wayward walkers in a bog.
Those lacking hats are often found
With minds that henceforth are unsound.
As you well know, the world agrees
That we must cover up our knees,
Our arms and elbows and our chest
With trousers, overcoat and vest.
Some people, though, do not provide
Protection from the countryside;
Then hatless, marching on a moor –
Careless, clueless and cocksure –
Expose their heads to wind and rain,
So they are never sane again.

Pyjama llamas

Said the leader of the llamas,
'Let us visit the Bahamas.
Where we'll don our pink pyjamas
To shade us from the sun.
They'll be pleased to see the grandees
From the awe-inspiring Andes.
To them we'll be the bee's knees
And a rare phenomenon.'

Great crowds were there to greet them;
The Mayor came out to meet them
And lavishly to treat them
On the golden-sanded shore.
They dined on bright bananas,
On rhubarb and sultanas –
And then they asked for more.

Said the leader of the llamas,
'We love their panoramas
And they our pink pyjamas,
So everyone is pleased.
Now Mr Mayor, we must be off.
We hear there's lots of food to scoff
In the Antipodes.'

The stolen shadow

The fat dictator, seeking to impress,
Stole the best shadow from his guardsmen's
      mess.
Shapely and sharply-edged, it was the kind
That one could spend a thousand years to
      find.
He gazed with glee that golden afternoon,
But retribution followed all too soon.
The disapproving sun refused to shine,
Blotting the tyrant's damnable design.

Dreaming

Let us slumber by the Humber,
Where the cool cucumbers grow;
Where no lumber will encumber
Drifting dreams that gently flow.

Let us think about relaxing
On this sunny summer day.
If our lives become too taxing,
Let us choose to sleep all day.

Richard III

The winter of his discontent
At last has run its race.
His bones all broken up and bent,
Lay underneath the thick cement
Of a car parking space.

King Richard was last seen alive
Way back in 1485.
He might have lived a little longer
Had his old steed been that bit stronger.
Like him it perished in the fight
That put the House of York to flight
And ended (not before its time)
The Wars of Roses pantomime.
In Dickie's Meadow on that day,
Events before the close of play,
Gave Shakespeare lots of famous lines
That send a shiver down our spines.
'A horse! A horse! my kingdom for a
        horse!'
Is known to everyone, of course.

Postscript

According to the leading boffin,
The king was buried without coffin;
And – lots of people think this worse –
The Tudors did not send a hearse.

Old men talking

That's right; I'm only eighty two.
I haven't lived as long as you.
Ninety, you say, and going strong.
I don't think I shall last that long.

Don't eat too much and never guzzle.
Solve each day a crossword puzzle.
Take brisk walks and keep a cat
Find a girlfriend for a chat.

Old friend, I love my fish and chips,
My easy chair, my racing tips.
And as for girls, I'm not like you.
I'm too far gone to bill and coo.

Nibbling

Let us nibble by the Ribble
Those big biscuits you have bought.
There is no cause to quail or quibble,
For any crumbs that drip and dribble
Will most easily be caught.

Cats and mice

Felines purr well by the Irwell,
Where unguarded mice are found.
Cool cats catch them and despatch
        them
With one swift and silent bound.

On the ball

If you plan to cross the Mersey,
Wear a fancy football jersey
Or a centre forward's shirt.
Like everyone on Merseyside,
You must take soccer in your stride
And be an extrovert.

Bacup

Bacup, oh, Bacup!
When will the world wake up
And give you a cheer?
Why is it no one sings
Of Stacksteads and of Irwell Springs,
Of Waterbarn and Weir?
Long gone your smoking mills.
Still stands your ring of hills,
Kingly and clear.

Higgs

Mr Higgs, the missing bo'sun,
Sits upon a driftwood plank.
He has floated on the ocean
Since the *SS Einstein* sank.
Searchers say that he's been sighted,
But it's very hard to tell.
Some believe he's been invited
To a costly Swiss hotel.

Coconuts

Wicked the brute who hurls a wooden ball
And laughs to see his helpless victim fall.
Wicked the showman in his shabby hut,
Who thrusts abasement on the coconut.
Vandals desist! Call off your vile attack
On food that has no means of fighting back.
The coconut deserves mankind's respect,
But you look on while its brave face is
       wrecked.

Take your pick

Some people purchase merchandise;
Others just go shopping.
Some people antisepticize;
Others call that mopping.

Rhubarb

'Rhubarb. Rhubarb,' said the actor,
Mouthing words he'd learned by heart.
His strong lines were the key factor
In the play's most telling part.
Those who heard him all remember
His rich 'Rhubarb's' golden glow;
How the word was like an ember;
How it shone and stole the show.

Anything goes

Writing light verses should always be fun.
(Remember that anything goes.)
Think of the fantasies experts have spun:
That adorable sports girl, Miss Joan Hunter
        Dunn,
And the Dong with Luminous Nose.

The cricketer

He was a very decent chap, his kindly vicar
     said.
He always liked to lend a hand;
His services were in demand;
He was fine spirited.

Cricket, the game he loved the best,
Took up much time; and he confessed
That through the years of married life,
He served his club more than his wife.
He marked the wicket, mowed the ground,
But though he practised, never found
The road to versatility.
And so he was obliged to be
A second teamer, number nine,
Who rarely had the chance to shine.
Yet once he made a splendid catch
To win a vital derby match,
And afterwards, when stretched by strain,
He'd say, 'I have not lived in vain.
I had my moment in the sun,
Though rarely did I score a run.'

The vicar said that he was sure
That selfless service would ensure
A just reward for our dear friend,
Who would receive a dividend
In keeping with his sporting love
On some fine cricket ground above.

'I think he'll make a mighty score,
At least a hundred runs or more.'

Now, when a batsman hits out freely,
Bowlers pay a heavy price.
Is the parson saying, really,
That there is pain in Paradise?
That, I'm certain, cannot be;
It falters as theology.
If you wish to be a winner,
First make sure you are a sinner.

Crowded

Simple Simon and the Village Idiot found all
the seats occupied when they boarded a
train. Along with many other travellers, they
had to stand. At each station a message
from the guard came over the loudspeakers:
'The company apologies for the crowded
conditions on this service. This is due to
there being a lot of passengers.'

'I'd never have thought of that,' said
Simon.

'Neither would I. It's very good of them
to let us know.'

Old MacDonald

Old MacDonald had a farm,
EE-I-EE-I-O.
But it was causing him alarm.
The failing business did him harm.
He made no money from his sheep.
The losses from his cows grew deep.
Things grew so bad he couldn't sleep.
He cried, 'Oh, no! Oh, no!'

Old MacDonald has a farm.
EE-I-EE-I-O.
It brings him in a tidy sum.
All troubles he has overcome.
His stock has gone, and in its place
The blades of tall wind turbines race.
How wise to change and to embrace
This source of instant dough.

Quiet diplomacy

When the Quakers met the bakers,
Nobody said a word.
That was the way the former worked,
Or so the latter heard.
The two were holding a review
About the price of pies.
The bakers felt it was askew;
They said so with their eyes.
The Quakers kept their hats on,
But underneath they smiled;
And then they nodded, all as one,
The bakers were beguiled.
And when the price of pies went up,
The Quakers all sat down,
Then, drinking from a loving cup,
They did not even frown.

Grave thoughts

Now let's put pockets into shrouds,
The undertaker said.
I'll guarantee that massive crowds
Will buy them for their dead.
Some people, as I'm sure you know,
Display their sense of pride
By making sure their loved ones go
With comforts by their side.
The grave's a fine and private place,
But better if one feels
The dear departed can embrace
Some token that appeals.
Think how the Pharaohs stocked their
      tombs
With objects beyond price:
Parasols and rich perfumes
Helped them to Paradise.
A pocket in a shroud could hold
A letter, let us say:
Warm words to overcome the cold
In that damp world of clay.

A fond farewell

Bury my toes at Shoeburyness
And my legs at Wounded Knee.
I'd like my departure to be a success
With a touch of flippancy.
Longsight will do for my failing eyes
And Waterfoot for my feet.
Please send, though it may cause
        surprise,
My heart to Chester-le-Street.
For my surplus fat, choose Medicine
        Hat;
And Cockermouth's right for my teeth.
When all's done and said,
Braintree for my head.
Now I've nothing left to bequeath.

Missed opportunity

The cuckoo in the cuckoo clock
Speaks out just once an hour.
Would he have ticked a better tock,
If he had greater power?
He could be paid to advertise
The joys of Alpine strolls
Or then again to idolize
The beauty of Swiss rolls.

Hiawatha's request

Hi! My name is Hiawatha
And I'm seeking information.
Tell me, please, what is a laptop?
I've been told that I could use one
In the comfort of my wigwam;
That I needn't send smoke signals
To my brother, Chibiabos
Or to lovely Minnehaha,
Also known as Laughing Water.
I am puzzled by this wonder.
It is hard to understand.
Light a fire and send a message.
I'll be watching from my land.

Easter, 2013

If this is spring, then roll on winter.
Christmas has a kinder face.
Wishing for the ice to splinter,
We all seek a warmer place.
Cricket soon will be upon us,
But the grounds lie under snow.
Why does Nature wish to con us?
Why this hypothermic blow?

Questions

Can anyone tell me? Does anyone know
Why it's raining so hard or when it will
     snow?
Why fields are bright green, but the sky's a
     bright blue?
Why water's so wet? Will you give me a
     clue?
Have thinking men found the real meaning
     of life?
And why is it wrong to eat peas with a knife?
Please drop me a line to help light up my
          lamp.
It costs fifty pence for a second-class stamp.

A true story

Anyone who tries to amuse his fellows with fiction runs the very serious risk of being outdone by real events; and to prove my point and to end this mishmash, I give the true story of a Lancashire girls' school speech day. The event took place long ago, but deserves to be remembered.

Picture the scene in the school hall: rows of uniformed young ladies to the front; their proud parents to the rear. On the platform the teachers in their gowns and the guest of honour, the local mayor. The headmistress says how honoured the school is to welcome the first citizen, whom she invites to hand out the prizes. Smiling broadly, His Worship begins,

When I were a lad at skoo, teitcher said to me, 'Amos, what dusti want to be when tha grows up?' An ah said, 'Please miss, Mur of Accrinton.'

Lightning Source UK Ltd.
Milton Keynes UK
UKOW031110120513

9 781907 197123